Just Call Me John

The Leadership Story of John Gagliardi

by

David J. Weeres, Ed.D.

NORTH STAR PRESS OF ST. CLOUD, INC.

St. Cloud, Minnesota

ISBN-10: 9-87839-356-0
ISBN-13: 978-0-87839-356-5

First Edition: May 2010

Printed in the United States of America

Published by
North Star Press of St. Cloud, Inc.
P.O. Box 451
St. Cloud, Minnesota 56302

northstarpress.com

JUST CALL ME JOHN

CONTENTS

ACKNOWLEDGMENTS

My sincere thanks
TO MY FAMILY

My wife, Karen, and our children, Ben and Heidi; you have been there for me, and that has made all the difference.

TO MY FATHER AND MOTHER

Arnold, the patience and wisdom you demonstrated to your youngest on the farm is my model for your grandchildren.

Mildred, as a young child I observed your finesse as a teacher in a one-room country schoolhouse. The vision is still fresh.

TO SAINT JOHN'S UNIVERSITY

To Saint John's University, the Alumni Department, the Athletic Department, those who responded to the survey, and particularly to the participants of this study. Without you, this work could not have been completed.

TO THE PHOTOGRAPHERS

John Biasi for photos on the front and back covers; to Saint John's University and the Gagliardi family for the remaining photos.

TO JOHN GAGLIARDI

For being who you are.

TO PEGGY GAGLIARDI

For telling us who John is.

TO MY EDITOR

To my father-in-law and personal editor, Jack Schneider. Your attempts to tutor me and edit my stories through the years have been deeply respected. Your expertise in producing a readable text has gained my deep appreciation.

TO MY TEACHERS

To all, thank you for your time. The knowledge you have shared is beyond measure.

TO BRANDY

To my golden retriever Brandy, who was at my feet daily, listened to my thoughts, and was there for every keystroke.

PREFACE

The origin of this volume took root in the research conducted for my doctoral studies. Somewhere along the way I knew I had a tale, a story much larger than an academic exercise. Since starting my dissertation, I have been asked by many people how the idea for this project originated or whether I have any connection with the subject. The fact is that I am not an alumnus of the university, nor a fanatical fan of its football program, nor had I ever met John Gagliardi (pronounced Guh-LAHR-dee).

At some point in the coursework for the doctorate, I was entertaining thoughts for a proper research project. It seems that many research works are done on problematic areas of our society; I decided to follow a different path. I chose to spend my time studying a positive problematic area, namely, to find something that appeared to be going well and to study it with a view toward helping others learn from its success. I was still deliberating on various topics when a moment came that we all hope for, and I snatched a thought that is like lightning in a bottle.

John Gagliardi, head football coach at Saint John's University at Collegeville, Minnesota, and record-holder of the most coaching wins in college football, had completed another successful season, and the local media coverage was dwindling at mid-winter (February, 2004). I had an intuition that there were facets of his character and his coaching that had not received the attention of the press, whether local or national. And so I made an appointment to see the coach in his campus office.

A snowstorm was pummeling the area as I arrived. I found my way to John's office and was invited to have a seat. Our conversation leapt from one topic to another and finally focused on leadership, a topic that seemed to heighten the coach's interest.

As we talked, different people stopped by the office and joined in the discussion. In the end, the office housed an eclectic group: a priest who was the athletic director, a long-time assistant coach, a current player, and four high school seniors on campus for a tour. John went out of his way to ask opinions of those present, engaging them in a practical, sometimes philosophical manner.

At moments during this conversation I was able to sit back and observe the interaction unfolding before me. Something was going on here in the interactions that was unexplainable at that moment, something unexpected, and I believed people were unaware of. Then a lightning strike: Has this coach affected his alumni beyond the game, with leadership implications? Have his players absorbed real-life lessons from his coaching?

And so it begins.

1

John Gagliardi

The Foundation

AS OF THE END OF THE 2009 SEASON, John Gagliardi completed his sixty-first season as a head coach of college football: four at Carroll College, Helena, Montana, and fifty-seven at Saint John's University, Collegeville, Minnesota. Yes, the story continues to evolve as he continues to coach. His college coaching career-record at the end of 2009 was 471 and 126 with 11 ties (.784), surpassing any other college football head coach in wins. His teams have earned four national championships: 1963, 1965, 1976, and 2003. According to John:

> I never thought I would do this. I came from immigrant parents, and all I ever heard as a kid was "Learn a trade." It was a way to get out of the coal mines. That's what my dad did. To get out of the coal mines, he became a blacksmith. He remained a blacksmith all his life and also opened a body shop. He became a body man. He taught my brother and opened a very nice body-shop business. I thought I was going to be a body man. That's what my brother did, my brother-in-law, my uncle, and that was a way to earn a living.

1

John began his coaching career in 1943, his senior year at Holy Trinity High School in Trinidad, Colorado. His high school football coach was called to serve in World War II, leaving the team without a coach. As John recalled:

It was a small school . . . you had the public high school and the Catholic high school. [John attended the Catholic high school.] Immediately when they talked about not having a football team at the Catholic high school, the public high school coach came running and tried to recruit me and a couple of the best players to his team. With my immigrant Catholic father, I know I'm not going to be able to go to the public school. He's not going to let me go there. He was a daily communicant. . . . I thought I would like to play that last year of football [as a senior]. I went to see the parish priest that ran the school. I said, "The coach over at the public high school wants most of us guys to transfer over to his school [they really only wanted two of them]." That scared the hell out of him. He said, "What should we do?" I said, "Why don't you let us try and run the team? I'm not thinking coach, but run it like an intramural team, just a bunch of guys get together and play." The priest asked me if I thought it would work. I said, "If we don't, we're going to lose these guys." That's all he had to hear. Maybe one guy might have gone; our parents would just never let us go. Football didn't mean anything to them. My dad would have been happy if I didn't play. I said to the priest, "Why don't you let us try it? You can come to a few practices and see how it is going. We can always cancel the schedule. . . ." Reluctantly he said yes. He came to the first couple of practices and then stopped coming.

We started the season, and we're winning. I was a backfield guy [kind of like a quarterback now] and learned from the year before. The year before we would call a play and nobody knew what they were doing. We would spend time in practice on long, thirty-

John in seventh grade, Trinidad, Colorado. (Courtesy of the Gagliardi family)

2

minute calisthenics, all kinds of drills. Then when we would call a play in the huddle and linemen would be asking me who to block. "Who do you block?!" I would say in the huddle. I've got the ball and getting killed because these poor guys don't know who to block. . . . I took over [the next year as a senior], and we would slowly figure it out [in practice] who they should block. We would hardly do any calisthenics. We asked if anybody wanted to do any calisthenics and they'd all say, "No, hell no!"

Our former coach was a traditional coach during practice and said "No water, you'll die." I didn't have any water because he didn't let you have any water. I always thought that was insane. [The myth at that time was that drinking water was dangerous during strenuous exercise.] So I remember, my senior year, after a couple of days I said, "The water fountain isn't that far away. I'm going to go get a drink." The guys looked at me and weren't going to get a drink. I went over there, took a drink, came back . . . and nobody moved. They didn't dare. They wanted to see if I was going to die because they believed it. So after a day or so they were all over by that fountain. There were a lot of little things like that. We were successful and won the championship the first time in school history.

The next year they don't have a coach yet. I'm running the body shop because everybody else is off to war, and the priest asks me to coach the football team. I can't leave because I'm the only guy over

John's senior year in high school, Holy Trinity, Trinidad, Colorado. (Courtesy of the Gagliardi family)

3

John on the left and Gene Gagliardi (a cousin) on the right. (Courtesy of the Gagliardi family)

there [at the body shop]. The priest says, "You can run the practices after work, 5:30 p.m." So that's what I did for another couple of years.

By the age of twenty Gagliardi had a high school football win/loss record of 31 and 12. He also played basketball in high school and at nearby Trinidad Junior College. John went on to say:

The basketball coach at the college [Jack Walton] . . . was the big break in my life. We played the junior college when we were in high school and we beat them, because they weren't really that good. When our high school season was over my senior year, the college sea-

John's high school graduation, 1944. (Courtesy of the Gagliardi family)

son was still going on. The college basketball coach asked me and my cousin to finish their season with them. We played another five or six games with them. To play with them, he enrolled us in a night typing class. We had to be registered with the college. I thought that was the end of it. [Graduated high school in the spring of 1944].

The next season [1944-1945] the college basketball coach asks me to play again. I told him I couldn't because I was the only one at the body shop. He said, "We could hold practice at six, after work,

Rose Ann (John's sister), John, and John's dad, Ventura, at the body shop. (Courtesy of the Gagliardi family)

so you could work, then come here. But you have to take a typing class and be a bona fide student." That was fine; I played that year with them.

Again, the next year he [basketball coach] wants me to play again. Everybody is back from the service, and now I'm the low man. These guys are all expert body men and I'm decent. The college coach says, "Why don't you come down here and talk. You would make a great coach. I've been watching you." That's the first time I even thought of making it a career. He says, "You're doing a good

6

John (on the far left), 1945, at Holy Trinity High School playing in Santa Fe. (Courtesy of the Gagliardi family)

job, but if you want to go into coaching, you've got to go to college." That was the first time that occurred to me. I never even thought of going to college. I thought that wasn't a bad idea, but I was a body man. I thought about it and brought my dad in to talk to the coach, and he says the same thing to him. After the coach leaves, my dad says to me, "You know, John, that's probably a good idea, with your brother back, and your brother-in-law, and your uncle it will be tough for all of us to earn a living and support a family. Maybe it would be better if you go to college." I felt kind of bad, because for a long time, a couple of years, I'm the only one in the body shop . . . I'm the guy! Now I'm the low man . . . . So I'm not really happy [pause], but yet kind of happy because it's college.

College wasn't really easy because I hadn't taken college prep courses because I didn't think I was going to college. A lot of times I thought college was kind of miserable. College is not easy, exams and all. Then I would think of the body shop, and think this is tough, but that was tougher. That used to help me, just thinking about it. . . . I was a good student, but not a great student.

In 1947 John enrolled at Colorado College and took over as the head football coach of nearby Saint Mary's High School. That year his team finished second in the conference and in 1948 won the conference title.

> I was away from home, no money, struggling financially, struggling in college. I was the only coach at Saint Mary's, which I loved. The only thing that would get me through it was thinking "This is a lot easier than being in that body shop." That used to help me a lot, thinking the alternative is tougher than this.

In the spring of 1949 John graduated from Colorado College, majoring in liberal arts. In the fall of 1949 he started coaching at Carroll College in Helena, Montana. He was hired to coach all sports (football, basketball, and baseball) and serve as athletic director. He coached there four years, compiling a record of 24 and 6 with 1 tie in football, with three conference titles and a .787 winning percentage. He became

John at Holy Trinity. (Courtesy of the Gagliardi family)

acquainted with all the area high school coaches while trying to recruit their players. Bill Osborne, a coach from Billings Central High School, was a Saint John's graduate and told John about an opening at Saint John's University.

> The Billings coach recommended me for the Saint John's job, and I got an interview. I really liked Carroll College and liked what I was doing, but I came out here [Saint John's], and they offered me a lot more money [$4,200 vs. $2,700 annually]. Saint John's was a bigger school, and as much as I hated to leave Carroll College, I did. Figured I was single and if it didn't work out, I'll be fine.
>
> The Billings coach had a passion for Saint John's University. I had never heard of Saint John's except for Bill. He was crazy about Saint John's. That kind of piqued my interest. I wished I thought that way about my college. I liked them but wasn't nuts about them. Ever since then I've noticed that most Saint John's men are that way. I've often thought to myself, What is it that these players are so rapturous about this place? . . . I don't know what it is, I don't have a clue. . . . The only other men I've ever heard the same about were the Notre Dame players. They are the same way. To this day I have never figured it out. It's hard to find a man that doesn't think it's a great place. I'm sure there are some, but I've never met one. . . . I don't know what it is.

I was sitting across the desk from John, staring into his eyes, not wanting to break the moment. I thought to myself, *When you're so close to the fire, you have a hard time seeing it for yourself.* And there it was, right in front of me, staring at me, one of many passionate fires on campus, right before me. John continued:

> They're proud men. I'm not one of them [Saint John's alumnus]. I think, What did I miss out on? You have to just marvel at it. . . . That's the way Bill Osborne was, so I thought it was worth a look.

In the fall of 1953 John began his coaching career at Saint John's University. He went on:

> When I came here, I discovered the coach leaving was Johnny Blood. He was a famous guy. After a couple days here, I knocked on his door and introduced myself and asked why he was leaving. He

said, "You can't win here. These monks are so tight, there's no way you can win here." He said he got ulcers; the monks didn't want to spend any money.

When I interviewed for the job, I was only twenty-six years old and not sure I really wanted the job. I liked where I was, I loved where I was. . . . I really liked coaching basketball; there was a basketball coach here. In the interview, there were about ten priests in the room, all in black robes. It was a different place then, with only five or six lay faculty. It was an entirely different place, no women. So they asked me, "Do you need scholarships?" I never had a scholarship personally, and at Carroll College we didn't have scholarships,

so I said "No, I don't think so." Then they asked, "Do you think you can beat Saint Thomas and Gustavus without scholarships?" I said, "We're winning at Carroll without scholarships. We beat some darn good teams, including Gonzaga in basketball. I was kind of naïve, really. I looked around, and the monks, sitting at a big table, were looking at each other, and I could see they were thinking "This is our guy." They didn't want to spend any money, and I was naïve enough to believe in it. And we did win! In retrospect, that was a naïve thing to do. Everybody else had scholarships, and we're the only ones without them. We held our own, but it was tough. When we went to Division III and no one had scholarships, we really started dominating. Everybody was on an even plane then.

John walking the sidelines at Saint John's, first year. (Courtesy of Saint John's University)

10

John's thoughts on why he was hired are undoubtedly partially correct. His "no scholarship" theory was a boost, but even at the age of twenty-six his win/loss record was impressive. He had coached at several Catholic high schools and was currently a coach at a small liberal arts Catholic college. This, combined with a recommendation from an alumnus, makes the historical picture clearer; John was an exceptional candidate by every standard.

In addition to football at Saint John's, John coached the track team until 1966 and was the school's hockey coach from 1955 to 1959. Regarding hockey, John said:

> The myth of my hockey coaching . . . After I was here a couple years, they lost the hockey coach, and they came to me and asked me to coach hockey. I don't even skate . . . . I went to one game while I was in college, didn't know a thing they were doing. I had only been to one game in my life! They said, "Why don't you just take it until we can get somebody else?" So I did. Seven years later I finally got out of it. My win percentage is still better than anybody else's here. . . . We didn't win a championship, because Duluth was in the league with the indoor rink. We did beat Duluth, but we had no business beating them. My point is, I coached basketball and transferred some of the skills but didn't know a thing about hockey. I coached track [at Saint John's] and won championships without ever having been out for track.
>
> Somehow I think I can handle men. You still have to have good ballplayers. You can't win without them. Somehow we have had decent players, and I don't think we screwed them up too much. I always had a sense of humor, kidding them. I've always sort of known how to do it. I'd like to think I know how to handle guys, I don't know why; I never took a course in it. I don't know how, but it worked out. I've always had a pretty good rapport with them, and I couldn't even tell you why or how.

On Family

ACCORDING TO JOHN'S WIFE, Peggy, there are several accounts of how they met. According to her:

Peggy Dougherty, 1952. (Courtesy of the Gagliardi family)

John picked up a student [Bob Verkuilen] who had an appendectomy [at the Saint Cloud Hospital]. I was walking with two girls toward town. It's a mile from the nurses' home to downtown, and the student knew the two other girls and they gave the three of us a ride uptown. John didn't even know I was in the car! John had to be so careful because he was a coach. John knew one of the girls because her brother was a baseball player and a football player. John said "Hi," but not another word. Verkuilen was very verbal and he did all the talking.

John and Peggy Dougherty had become acquainted through a mutual friend, and then one day . . . Peggy continued:

I was going into my senior year [nursing school], and I met him downtown, and he asked if I wanted a Coke. I said "Sure" [pause]. I was looking for that ride home, that's what I was looking for! That mile is exhausting! He then asked me if I wanted to go to a picnic. We dated for about one month, and then he went home for the summer [Colorado]. . . . He came back with a diamond ring!

12

John and his parents, Ventura and Antoinette. (Courtesy of the Gagliardi family)

John and Peggy raised their four children in a house that still stands on the edge of the campus: Nancy, Chisago City, Minnesota; John Jr., Hudson, Wisconsin; Gina, Becker, Minnesota; and Jim, Saint Cloud, Minnesota. They have lived there all but the first year of their married life. Jim discussed growing up:

> We would play the typical night games like kick the can, and my friends would want my dad to play. He was a great dad to have in the neighborhood. I don't know how he didn't get sick of everyone over at our house all the time.

13

John and Peggy at their wedding on Valentine's Day, 1956. (Courtesy of the Gagliardi family)

There was only one time when John seriously considered leaving Saint John's University. The year was 1983, and the University of San Diego was interested in him. They flew John and Peggy to San Diego for a visit. Peggy said: "It was February and the weather was beautiful. They had even found us a place to live." They had an inclination to

14

Peggy with John, Jr., Nancy, and Gina. (Courtesy of the Gagliardi family)

accept the job on the spot. The weather was a natural draw compared with the normal Minnesota February. John and Peggy discussed the move and then, according to Peggy, John said, "Let's go home first."

Back home in Minnesota it was widely known that John was considering the San Diego position. According to Peggy, the monks at Saint John's did an admirable job of shielding John from a continuous barrage of phone calls from Saint John's supporters and sports media personnel. In the end it was family ties that kept John at Saint John's. Peggy continued:

> We are really a close family. John's family is in Colorado and mine is scattered. So there was just our little family, with the four children. We won't see these kids if we move. Two were already married and another one was close. The kids wouldn't be able to afford to come see us very often. We both decided [to stay], but it was his choice, and I'd go if he wanted to.

Gina, John, Jr., Jim, Nancy, John, and Peggy, 1983. (Courtesy of the Gagliardi family)

They had a big banquet for him; I think half of Saint Cloud was there. When they have something like that, he hates it, because he says, "Who's going to show up?" It was unbelievable! They were thanking him for staying. He's a real family person. When his grandkids come, he drops everything. One of them, a toddler, says "Grumpa come!" And John runs.

Peggy continued about John's oldest friends and his family:

His group of guys in Trinidad [Colorado] went through grade school and high school together. They all went to different colleges. They're close-knit and kept up with each other. They'll be on the phone for an hour talking. We used to go back to Colorado every summer, mid-June till the first part of August. I don't know what his poor mother did; she must have been an angel when I think of it now.

John and family playing games. (Courtesy of the Gagliardi family)

John's long-time assistants have all been former players of his: Jim Gagliardi as offensive coordinator; Jerry Haugen as defensive coordinator; Gary Fasching and Brandon Novak as assistant coaches. Jim said, "It's like working for the family business. I enjoy it. I get to see him every day."

In the Gagliardis' early years at Saint John's, there weren't many laymen on the staff. Peggy found this to have benefits and humorous drawbacks. She related:

> Early on when John and I were dating, I would go to his office for a visit. It seems every time I went, Father Adelard was there. He was a good friend of John's and would spend some time in his office. John and I took a trip to the Cities to see a movie. Finally I had John to myself! We drove to the Cities together, just got to the theater, and then guess who shows up? Father Adelard! He was down there for something else and needed a ride home. It was like a double date!

The family listening to John's speech, 1983. (Courtesy of the Gagliardi family)

In recent years John and Peggy purchased a very modest lake home not far from campus. Peggy told how that came to be:

> We spent every summer out here [at the lake]. We would bring the boat out and then bring it back to the house. The kids loved it. Brother Mark [Kelly]—he's kind of like a brother to John—had a boat. He would bring us out here and we would go out in his boat. He would pull the kids on skis, and he was so patient with them. He never stopped till they got up on those skis. We would eat on his boat. The kids loved this lake.

Jim once saw a house for sale on the lake. Peggy wanted to look at it, but John was reluctant. They had lived in the house at Saint John's since 1956. They did finally look at the lake house. Peggy said:

I was so hopeful, but I thought there was no way. . . . When we left the house, John said that it was "nice, but not for us." The next morning we woke up and he says, "Peggy, would you like that place?"

He would do anything for me. For himself he doesn't need anything. If I didn't buy his clothes for him, he would have his underwear from fifty years ago! I was born and raised on lakes. We go down to the pontoon and just sit and have a cold drink now. He just loves it out here now.

We can't discuss family and ignore the Catholic Benedictine family that surrounded John and Peggy, especially in the early years. John lived in the dorms during his years at Carroll College and then again for several years at Saint John's. John talked about the monks' influence:

Even in high school the boss was a priest. . . . One was an assistant coach and later became president of the college [Carroll], then bishop, and then archbishop of Seattle. He's retired now. I was privileged to be with some men that were out of my league. At Carroll I ate with the priests and started working closely with them. There were some great guys there, and there were some great men here. I would say there were some great men in both places. I got to be friends with them. They were not all my type, but a lot of them were. Intellectually, most of them were out of my league.

Jim Gagliardi discussed growing up on the Saint John's campus:

We grew up in an interesting place. I didn't even notice it, but it must have been like part of the family. I know it had an effect. There's probably a sense that the monks were watching out for us and we were all sharing this home like a big family.

Early in his career at Saint John's, John held film sessions of the previous week's game for the monks. During these years, over two hundred monks lived on campus. Of the film sessions, John said:

There was no TV for them, and they didn't leave campus much. It was a good way for me to meet with them, and they were very interested. They'd have a big classroom full of them. It was very good, but kind of dangerous because they were right on top of the scene (John considered them to be his boss). I enjoyed it a lot.

The priests and brothers were John and Peggy's friends and extended family for much of their life. From the previous stories we can catch a glimpse of the daily influence, but it is doubtful that any of us can truly comprehend the positive influence of this extended family in its entirety.

"As a coach we're always trying to build up their confidence."
—John Gagliardi

On Winning, Losing, and Disconnecting

IN JOHN'S OFFICE, no more than a couple feet from his desk, in front of many books on a bookshelf, sits a picture. It is four inches by five inches in size, black and white, unframed. John talked about it:

John's kids at the concession stand while he was fighting for his life down on the football field. (Courtesy of the Gagliardi family)

I can disconnect. I'm pretty good at that. I think that is how I survived. First of all, when I had a young, growing family, I would try to give them some quality time. It was great for me, too, because I enjoyed being around them. See that little picture there of those two little guys? I've kept that there for years to try and remind myself . . . this is at a football game, these are my two oldest when they were young. I'm sure I was down on the field fighting for what I thought was life or death, and they were interested in whether they could get some popcorn at the concession stand. They could care less what was going on. On the field, win, lose, they would be the same, happy to see me. I enjoyed that. It took my mind off the game.

Sometimes it's not easy to take a bitter loss. I enjoyed it a lot more when we won. . . . If you watch a Saturday game, one team is elated and the other is in the depths of despair, like there is a death in the family. I don't know why they take it so bad, but they really do. The amazing thing I've noticed with coaches is the highs are nice, but the lows don't seem to be equal. It's like looking at a graph. The highs are nice, but the lows seem to go off the board; you can't go any lower. And it is still that way with me. Why should I really worry? I've broken the records, I'm not going to get fired. Because you had to worry about that, look at these poor coaches that got fired this week. . . . It's a tough business. It just doesn't feel good when you lose.

I tried to think happy thoughts, forced myself to try and forget the bad things. I tell my players and I try to practice this myself. I can easily give the advice a lot easier than taking it myself. . . . You have to flush the toilet and walk away from it. . . . You have learned from your mistakes. It's going to happen to everybody. You're going to have some real downers. . . . The simple thing is to just forget it and move on to the next task. And the beautiful part about coaching is, after about a day or so of working on the next business, if you really throw yourself into it, you don't even know who you played last week. It is all forgotten because you can't think of two things at one time. If you keep thinking about that next job, you can't think of that last one. After about two weeks you can't remember anything about it. . . . Work, I think, is a wonderful thing because, if you're really throwing yourself into it, you can't dwell on the past.

The other thing is if you have a great triumph, like a win, and you keep dwelling on that and celebrating. That's a pitfall, too, because now you're not getting ready for the next team, and that's when you get beat. You didn't do enough preparation because you were doing too much celebrating or constantly thinking of how wonderful it was. So now you don't think about the next challenge, and you are susceptible to a loss then.

It's important to get the players focused on the next opponent. If they're celebrating how great it was last week, you've got to get them to focus. What you've got to be really careful of is when you had a bitter upset. . . . Now, the biggest mistake you can make is to pound them and keep on them. That's the one where you have to immediately start building them back up. Don't, for God's sake, don't be hard on them. They feel bad enough, they're all human. Don't be knocking them down. When they're winning, you can do anything to them.

I've heard some coaches say they have to break them. How the heck, [pause] don't they know what the word "break" means? You've got to build them up, just the opposite. As a coach, we're always trying to build up their confidence.

I think you've got to be very careful in games where people think you're going to pound them. You have to be very careful. It's dangerous. . . . Games are won in the preparation more than anything. You have to work intelligently, prepare intelligently. Take away what they do best. How do you know what they do best? You have to study it. You have to focus on what they do.

Football is a game and anything can happen. You may have done everything properly, but the ball bounces the wrong way or the officials make a bad call. So now you have to overcome it. I always say the anatomy of an upset is this: You come up against somebody you should beat pretty easily. You know it. They know it. This team comes in thinking they don't have a chance, but they're going to give it everything they've got. They're going to do everything they can, and they get a break, something happens and they get a real break. . . . They start to think they're okay, and then they get another break. Now, if they get on top of you, your team starts crumbling and they get off rhythm. The other team—it's like a fire. They are getting stronger, and then more things happen and just like that you have a tremendous upset! That happens every week to somebody. That's the way it is because you've got human beings playing each other.

John continued with his thoughts on how to get control of an upset in progress.

Shake it off. Don't let that bother you too much. As we always say, shake it off as quick as you can. Don't dwell on it. Let's say you threw an interception or fumbled or had a penalty or whatever. You can't keep festering on it and thinking about it, annoyed at yourself or somebody else. You've got to bounce back, shake it off. It's not easy to do; you have to just fight through it. The way to fight through it is to not think about it. Think happy thoughts, as simple as that is. Think of the good things. Try to see the bright side of everything. If you keep dwelling on the negative, I think that is when everything collapses, it gets worse. But even at that, sometimes it doesn't work out. After all, the other team is pretty darn good. A lot of times they're just better than you are, and you can't do anything about it. They're doing things that make them a great team too. If they beat you, you just have to shake that off and get ready for the next one.

John revealed one of his greatest fears:

I was always worried, and still am, that we'd go through a whole season without winning a game. Unfortunately, that happens to people. I don't know how we got on to that conversation [with Father Adelard]. Maybe talking about our fears. After every game [first win of the season] he'd say to me, "This is not the year." Thank God! That was one of my greatest fears [pause] and still is. I'm not out of the woods here. As long as you coach, you can get embarrassed.

Jim Gagliardi discussed coaching with his dad and said, "I've never seen a person more fearful of losing." Discussing John's greatest fear, Jim says, "You kind of chuckle when he says it, but it's absolutely serious."

Losing doesn't happen very often and statistically has become more rare through the decades. John Gagliardi's football coaching record at Saint John's University is as follows:

1953 to 1959: 38 wins, 18 losses, 1 tie (.675 winning percentage)
1960 to 1969: 65 wins, 21 losses, 3 ties (.747 winning percentage)
1970 to 1979: 70 wins, 20 losses, 2 ties (.772 winning percentage)
1980 to 1989: 71 wins, 25 losses, 2 ties (.735 winning percentage)
1990 to 1999: 96 wins, 17 losses, 2 ties (.843 winning percentage)
2000 to 2009: 107 wins, 19 losses, 0 ties (.849 winning percentage)

"In some ways nothing has changed, and yet everything has changed."
—John Gagliardi

Change

JOHN SPOKE OF THE CHANGES he has seen in his six decades of coaching.

I used to think that the most miraculous thing was the correctable typewriter. . . . Now look what they've done with spell check and such. But some things are basic, just like football. You still have to think, write, and create. You have to slowly evolve.

The bad part about it is, if I can say there is anything negative, we have more players now, a squad of 170. You don't get to know them like when we had a squad of fifty or sixty. . . . I have too many assistants. At one time you were alone, you did the whole thing. I had a lot to do with everybody. I taped their ankles . . . you really got to know them pretty well. There are some players now I don't even know or recognize. That part I don't like at all. . . . I've delegated so much out now. The players all used to come see me. Now they go see their various coaches. Is that good or bad? I don't know, but it is different. You are getting almost like a CEO of a big corporation with people doing things. As a one-man operation I knew everything and knew everybody.

We really shouldn't have as big a squad as we do because it is inefficient. But I figure if these players want to be part of this and stay with us, they're paying big bucks, and if they get something out of it, that's great. If they don't see me, they see other coaches and other players. It's like a big family.

I used to do all the recruiting; I was the only guy. Now my assistants do a lot of the initial work. I see the students when they come for a campus visit. . . . I don't know whether it's good or bad, it's just different.

I can go back to when I thought film and projectors were just great . . . .We've had some drastic changes. It's this computer stuff, the way we look at films. Everybody [competitors] is taking ten steps forward. If we had that advantage and they didn't, it would be a different ballgame. . . . It's change, and you've got to change with it. I think the big thing is we've been somehow able to stay with it, especially when we were changing from film to video tape. I had a heck of a time dragging the rest of the coaches in the conference. I think I've been in the forefront, even with all these younger coaches in the conference, with change. I don't know what that is saying—it is still work and you've got to show up and do it; it doesn't do itself. You can have all these tools, but if you don't use them, it doesn't do anybody any good. These films—even though we have this modern stuff, it doesn't analyze itself. Then you still have to present it to the team and plan to work it out. It is still basically the same. It's kind of like writing. Sure, you have a computer with a spell checker, but somebody has to have the thought to put it down.

Years ago, on Saturday, we would put the game film on a bus to Minneapolis, where they would process the film. It was a big process. But that was better than going to Duluth and trying to scout them year after year and killing yourself. We would try to send somebody to scout, and if there wasn't anybody, I'd do it myself. Now we've gotten to the point where we send it through the Internet. We swap every film now. That's hard to believe. There is so much data going out, it's overdone. They always said the computer is going to lessen work. I don't think so. It has increased the work because you have more information to process. I loved it when we didn't have any films, didn't scout anybody. I enjoyed it. We used to have a lot of coffee breaks. I would go over and have coffee breaks all the time, maybe an hour [with faculty and students]. It was really a nice deal. Now I don't even meet with our own guys. We're busy all day . . . they're all busy. If you come here on a weekday, we hardly see each other. I don't know if that's good or bad. It's just different.

People don't change. You have basically good people. I've never dealt with the ones that aren't; they don't let them in this place (Saint John's). They're not perfect—they haven't removed the confessionals yet.

In some ways nothing has changed, and yet everything has changed.

Peggy continued the thought of change. For many years she worked in the nursing field: delivery, emergency, nursing home, and instructor in the Saint Ben's nursing program, filling in for several years for a professor on sabbatical. When the professor returned, Peggy found her way once again at John's office. Peggy said, "I've loved every job I've had." She worked for several years as an unpaid administrative assistant to John. She was eventually hired by the university in the 1980s for administration duties in the athletic department and stayed there until retiring in June 2005.

Peggy on change:

> When I first got there and the phone would ring [there were nine coaches using one line], and no one wanted to answer the phone. They wanted John to answer it because it was always for him. Then John would answer it, and it would be for someone at the other end of the hall. They have finally switched to separate lines now. John answers his own phone, even now.

John continued:

> People always ask me about changes. I guess there have been a lot of changes; a lot longer hair, bib overalls, tattoos, piercing—of course—that's just the faculty.

"Just keep on keeping on."
—John Gagliardi

The Routine

THERE IS A ROUTINE TO THE WORK of coaching. Depending on the season, the routine changes. During the fall season it is game time; in winter and spring recruiting is done; and in summer film, equipment, and structures, including the field of play, undergo maintenance. John discussed the routine during the football season:

> It is almost the same every week. In preparing for new games and making adjustments to differences. . . . No two teams are the same,

but yet they are all the same. . . . There are slight variations in preparations.

I show up every day, a little before 8:00 a.m. I'm not one of those guys that are here all night; we work hard all day. Then at practices—we have short practices, one and a half hours and we're out of here; it's probably 6:30 p.m. But then I go home; I've always gone home. We don't stick around much beyond that. We try not to work on Sundays. Come Sunday afternoon I and another coach [Jim] prepare the game film, and the rest of the coaches stay home. We're probably one of the only teams in the country that doesn't really work on Sundays. We've done that for years and haven't changed. We haven't changed, because we keep winning. If we weren't winning, we would have to do something different.

That's strange we say nothing is different. Within the same hours everything is different. The tools and preparations for each team are all different. We have different players, and every four years the whole campus is gone. . . . Every year a quarter of the campus turns over. We're doing it, but so is everybody else. So after a number of years you see these guys go on to become—well, one is a bishop in Cleveland. They're all over the map. It's amazing, and I always marvel at what they are doing.

It's a simple deal: you just keep working on the next project, and before you know it sixty years have gone by. People ask about burnout, and I really don't even know what that means. I just keep doing what I'm doing, and before long it amounts to a lot of years. Every day you just do the job. Just keep on keeping on.

Peggy told a slightly different story to me at mid-winter (2009):

Do you see those cards on the window sill? I find those cards all over the house with plays on them. He doesn't relax much during the season. After a game he is just exhausted. Then he is just climbing the walls by 2:00 p.m. on Sundays because he can't wait to get in the office. Even during the summer he'll put a film in and watch it. He sees things nobody else sees.

When we go out he never talks football. If someone asks him a question, he'll talk about it though. He loves business, and to talk about it. He gets books for Christmas—some football, but a lot of business.

"Practices are a little like a classroom—you're teaching."
— John Gagliardi

Nonconforming Teaching Methods

JOHN IS WIDELY KNOWN for some unusual coaching methods, perhaps the most distinctive of which is "no tackling in practice." According to John, "I never really believed in a lot of tackling in practice." Referring to Trinidad High School, he said, "We always had a limited number of guys. Senior year in high school we didn't tackle much." Arriving at Saint John's, John had an assistant coach who was older, and old school, and he believed in more tackling in practice. John recalled an incident in the 1950s: "We hurt a key guy in practice, and that was it."

John explained how some of his other theories developed:

> Practices are a little like a classroom—you're teaching. How are you going to teach if everybody is so miserable and cold or if it is raining? I've always respected lightning! Same with the gnats. How can you practice with those bugs tormenting you? We can go inside and do pretty much what we do outside. We're not going to tackle anyway. It's a little harder on the legs and feet. We've had guys standing outside, they were just torn apart with so many mosquito bites. We had one poor kid, we had to take him to the hospital. We just figured, this is ridiculous.

As for blocking sleds and short practices, John discussed time management. He said he would rather spend the time on running plays than using blocking sleds. And as for shorter practices, he asked, "How long can you hold someone's attention?"

Regarding wearing football cleats and using whistles as a coach, John said:

> I about killed myself on these floors [slippery on hard surfaces]. So I quit wearing them early in my career. Same with the whistle; I don't think you have to scream and holler at guys to get their attention. They seem to know. That's just the way we do it.

2

John's Players Speak

Saint John's

FOR HOME FOOTBALL GAMES on Saturdays in the fall, the campus swells with fans. Since 2001 the Johnnies have led the Division III home attendance records, averaging 47,000 fans annually, or 7,200 fans per home game. Clemens Stadium is surrounded on three sides by hills; on the steepest one is seating for the home crowd. The stadium is ringed for the most part by beautiful fall foliage.

The first building on what is now the campus of Saint John's was made of stone from the area in 1866. Today the abbey church, which is of modern design and construction, stands near that spot. The campus also houses a preparatory school, a liturgical publishing house, a pottery studio, a school of theology, an ecumenical institute, a manuscript library, a science hall, an athletic complex, dormitories, an arboretum, and a large brick quadrangle housing classrooms and offices, among others. The 2,400 acres of mostly forest and lakes add an element of seclusion to the campus.

Saint John's, first known as Saint Louis on the Lake, was founded by five Benedictine monks who left Saint Vincent Abbey in Latrobe, Pennsylvania, for Minnesota in 1856. They first settled in Saint Cloud but later moved to an area known as Indianbush, now home to Saint John's Abbey and University at Collegeville.

Saint John's University and the College of Saint Benedict (CSB/SJU) merged as a Catholic liberal arts university in 1988. The two colleges, six miles apart, are intertwined in many ways. Saint John's, located at Collegeville, Minnesota, is an all-men's campus; Saint Benedict's, located in Saint Joseph, Minnesota, is an all-women's campus. The two campuses share a common curriculum, degree requirements, and campus calendar. The combined enrollment for both campuses is about four thousand students.

The university's vision is to cultivate within each student a lifelong search for wisdom. Each department's mission is grounded in the Benedictine tradition. The monastery on the campus at Saint John's University influences all facets of campus life.

To Lead, in a Benedictine Tradition

How does one really know how good a leader one is? If we base that question only on a win/loss record, we have lost our way. A leader's job is to lead an organization. One of the more important and difficult skills of leading is to mentor followers and develop them into leaders themselves. It is difficult to lead; it is even more difficult to train your followers to become leaders. John philosophizes: "I don't know if I have much advice to give to anybody. If somebody picks up something along the way, that kind of astounds me."

And so, this is where we started. Has John developed his followers into leaders, and if so, how? What can we learn from the Johnny alumni who played football under John Gagliardi's coaching?

Alumni

With approximately fifty players on the roster each year in John's early years at Saint John's, choices for those who had something to say about John were many. As the decades progressed, the roster grew substantially. There were approximately 150 to 185 on the roster each season from 2000 to the present.

These alumni who speak about John in the second half of the book include men who had been quarterbacks, receivers, offensive and defensive linemen, a running back, and a linebacker. The undergraduate degrees these men earned ran a broad range, including English, Economics, Accounting, Business, Political Science, Social Science, and Communications. The question asked of these former players was: Did John Gagliardi impact individuals profoundly and how did he influence their subsequent lives?

"It is more of what the team achieves."
—Mike Grant

Mike Grant (class of 1979) went on to become a successful teacher, coach, and activities director at Eden Prairie High School in Minnesota. Mike stated: "It is more of a culture he [John Gagliardi] creates that we are all in this together. He creates that through storytelling, through his actions . . . it is all about the team and Saint John's." John does not bestow individual awards or pick a most valuable player (MVP) at the end of the season. In fact, all seniors take turns in bearing the title "captain" on game days. John feels that "picking an MVP is like picking your favorite child. Whoever you're with, that's your favorite." Since taking over in his present position, Mike has followed John's example and eliminated individual awards and MVP status.

The team concept came up again and again. Jeff Korsmo (class of 1980), an offensive tackle, who is currently executive director of the Mayo Clinic Health Policy Center in Rochester, said, "It's not just the

Jeff Korsmo. (Courtesy Jeff Korsmo)

twenty-two guys that start on the football team." Reserves are used in practice sessions to mimic an opposing team's plays and tendencies. He continued:

Whether I was third or fourth string or the starter, I felt I had a role to play. . . . It isn't about you; it's about the program. . . . The experience with John was a great preparation for our organization [medical care]. Each of us has an important role to play on the team. . . . There are plenty of organizations that produce people that, if their name isn't the one in the front of the headline or the one touted as the best, . . .

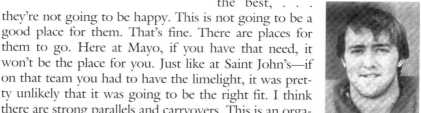

Korsmo in 1979. (Courtesy Saint John's University)

they're not going to be happy. This is not going to be a good place for them. That's fine. There are places for them to go. Here at Mayo, if you have that need, it won't be the place for you. Just like at Saint John's—if on that team you had to have the limelight, it was pretty unlikely that it was going to be the right fit. I think there are strong parallels and carryovers. This is an organization that for all the fantastic medical people you don't read a lot of names in the newspaper. What you read about is the Mayo Clinic and the team approach.

Respect for others was another recurrent theme voiced by former players. It embraced respect for teammates, opponents, professors, women, and Saint John's University. Jeff Korsmo put it this way: "Treat people as you would want to be treated." John Gagliardi emphasized this thought: "We don't have a lot of rules, just one—the Golden Rule: Treat everybody the way you want to be treated."

During an early interview with Brandon Novak (class of 2000), a memorable moment in his life was discussed, namely, the first time he met John Gagliardi. Brandon came to John's office with a friend, and the conversation had very little to do with football. In fact, John spoke to Brandon's friend in his native Spanish language. What I found unusual about this was the fact that John was not doing a hard sell of the football program and all the success it has had over the years. He was more interested in the people visiting him and learning about them as people rather than talking

Brandon Novak. (Courtesy Saint John's University)

about his own success. Brandon said, "It's about relating to people. He's a master at that." Brandon is currently the head wrestling coach and assistant football coach at Saint John's University.

Many people mentioned this aspect of John's initial interviews. John was interested in his players and their families—where they were from, what they wanted to do, what their parents did for a living. John would take this time in the interviews to promote the university and the quality education each person would obtain at Saint John's. These discussions had little to do with the coach's winning program and everything to do with the young men with whom he was speaking.

Fred Cremer (class of 1967), an offensive and defensive tackle who became a high school English teacher and coach in Illinois, had this to say about his first impression of John Gagliardi: "I found here [at Saint John's] this guy—soft-spoken, doesn't look like a football coach, and doesn't look like an athlete." As they walked around the campus, John talked about the buildings being kind of sparse and old. Fred then quoted John as saying, "It's not the buildings that make the school, it's the people." Fred then said, "I thought about that for a long time and still do.

Fred Cremer (number 75) in action. (Courtesy Saint John's University)

What he was saying was that this was a quality place, and if you come here, you will have a wonderful experience, which I did." Fred went on to say: "The conversation was dominated by other things, not football. It was all about the education at Saint John's, Minnesota, being out in the country, with the woods and lakes, totally not what I was expecting." Even in recent years, whenever Fred stopped by for a visit, the conversation was "three percent about football and ninety-seven percent about whatever—global warming, European economy, not football. John doesn't want to talk about himself and all his awards; he would rather talk about us and our families. He is diverting the attention away from himself." Mike Grant said, "He [John] does not talk about his intellect or ability but about the great young men he has had to coach."

Kurt Ramler (class of 1997), head football coach at Carleton College, Northfield, Minnesota, described a visit to the campus:

It was a pretty big surprise. You hear about the legendary coach, and kids call him John. He's laid back, smiling, kind of goofy in a great way, more human than you expected. When you walk away from his office, you think of him smiling.

John Agee. (Courtesy John Agee)

John Agee tackling an opponent in 1969. (Courtesy Saint John's University)

John Agee (class of 1970), currently president of Carlson Holdings, Minnetonka, Minnesota, suggested that John has respect for people and wants to learn about them. "It's all about whoever John Gagliardi is speaking to. That is why he understands talent so well—because he really gets to know people." Applying this to his business, Agee said:

> I have hired lots and lots of people over the years, and it is really important to understand who they are. . . . Sizing up people you put

John and some of his staff at a game. (Courtesy John Biasi)

Joe Mucha (class of 1966). (Courtesy Joe Mucha)

money with is very critical to understanding who they are, and it's getting them to open up and speak to you on a personal level. I think John Gagliardi is a master at that.

Of his first meeting with John Gagliardi, Tom Linnemann (class of 2000), business executive at Target Corporation, recalled:

It was not businesslike, not a hard sell or promises you don't believe. I think you can see through phony on a certain level, and John wasn't. He really wanted me to be there. He was very sincere; I could see myself developing a relationship with him.

This principle of respect for people as individuals was demonstrated to Joe Mucha (class of 1966) at a banquet:

> John would acknowledge and recognize third and fourth stringers at a banquet. We expected him to know about the starters, but to know the third and fourth stringers was memorable. Why would you know third and fourth stringers and beyond? That's work! He enjoys this process immensely, and it had a good impression on the starters.

Joe Mucha in action. (Courtesy Saint John's University)

Mucha applied this concept of recognizing the individual person before the player in his management career as he rose to vice-president of human resources at General Mills. This former player attempted to get to know people up and down the hierarchy of a large organization. "Everyone is treated with the same respect, from CEO to administrative assistants. Whether talking to the chairman of the board or an administrative assistant, I would view them as people, not their status."

Mucha went on to say:

> In the beginning [of a management career] it was like a pyramid, and you were on the top, commanding down. Then the pyramid turned and I was on the bottom, saying, "How can I help enable them [the employees] to achieve the organization's goals?"

Adam Herbst during his football years.
(Courtesy Saint John's University)

Adam Herbst (class of 1999). (Courtesy Adam Herbst)

John Gagliardi did this by allowing leadership to develop and flourish within several subgroups of players. These leaders come forth from the group in an unformulated way and are given great latitude of command during games.

As a State Farm Insurance agent, Adam Herbst (class of 1999) discussed being promoted to management:

> You cannot have them [the employees] conform to everything you do, nor should they, because there are a lot of different ways to get to the same end result. As long as the customer is being taken care of . . . then we're all right. That was a struggle for me initially getting into a management role, kind of letting go, letting them do their job, letting them use the skills they have, not watching over them and micromanaging them. That is what John does well. That is what good leaders do: they give people the ability to make decisions to do their jobs, and then they get the hell out of the way.

During the week leading up to game day, starting offensive and defensive players were typically divided for practice. Each group watched game films of opponents and practiced plays that the coaching staff deemed to be successful. On the offensive side, the quarterback was the logical choice as leader, but not the only one. During game week, the coaching staff would submit new plays and variations of old plays for the weekly practice sessions. A rough game plan was formulated on offense and defense according to perceived strengths and weaknesses of the next opponent.

Once the game began, play-calling was left up to the experienced quarterback. This was not an occasional audible at the line of scrimmage but a continuous string for the game. Quarterbacks thrust

Bernie Archbold (class of 1958). (Courtesy Saint John's University)

into the game because of injury were helped with play-calling from the sideline, but only for a limited time; they were expected to run the offense with little help from the sideline once the game was underway.

Bernie Archbold, a quarterback in the class of 1958 and later district agent for Northwestern Mutual Life Insurance, who passed away in 2008, had said in his interview: "[John] gave full rein to whoever was out there to let them play the game." Occasionally, plays were sent in from the sideline, according to Bernie and another quarterback, Kurt Ramler. Then again, a play would be sent in from John or the other coaches, and "as funny as it may sound, it would be a suggestion," according to Denny Schleper (class of 1983), executive principal at LarsonAllen LLP). Tom Linnemann (class of 2000) confirmed this operating philosophy with a comment that sideline plays were a "suggestion." Schleper put it this way: "The offense would decide quickly whether to run the play or not, and he [John] was always okay with that. You saw players really step up and become leaders." From the graduation dates of these quarterbacks one can witness that this philosophy has been in operation for an extensive time.

Fred Cremer, a lineman said, "There was ownership of the team by everyone. Players had the ability to change things, make suggestions." There would be conversations on the sideline with the players and the coaches during the game and at halftime, but the game was fundamentally in the hands of the players once underway. Kurt Ramler conjectured that this philosophy may have contributed to John's success: "The defense [of opponents] has to adjust to a new quarterback, not a long-term [predictable] coach calling plays. The offense has been more varied over the years."

Bernie Archbold was asked if he thought this independence on the field carried over to his life as a district agent for Northwestern Mutual Life in Marshall, Minnesota. "Emotionally I think it did, psychologically I think it did. I felt kind of good about the responsibility that John entrusted to me. . . . I felt okay then with taking responsibility, with running a business and helping young people succeed."

Adam Herbst discussed this independence in football terms and current business terms: "The employees, or football players, like it, and it makes them feel good about coming to work every day."

Denny Schleper had a recent discussion with John, who said, "I do my best job when I'm not doing anything." This referred to the assistants John hired to work with him day to day. "If you put the right people in place, you have to get comfortable with not doing anything. But you did your thing by putting those people in place." As Denny has risen in a large organization, from hands-on, task-oriented status to supervision and administration of a large group of employees, he said he "thinks of that quite often."

Another perspective on this considers the concept of how individuals fit into an organization: Are they forced into a position, or do they have free will and are able to find the path for themselves? John Gagliardi touched on this topic:

> It's always amazing how you have just the right number of people at positions. I've thought about that. We don't go after a center or other positions, although sometimes for a quarterback we will. If you get a

team of twenty-four or forty, you always get the right number per position. Sometimes you have to move them, but generally, somehow they arrive at the right spots; they figure it out themselves. I always tell the story of a great receiver we had. This guy is a little guy, receiver. We have this conference meeting of coaches, picking all-conference players, and this coach, a good guy, said to me "I've got to give you credit. You got this player right out from under our nose. He played quarterback in high school and we looked at him and figured he couldn't play quarterback; he was too small and couldn't throw the ball. You get him and move him to wide receiver and he kills us! For three years he kills us!" I didn't say anything to the coach. I come back and called the kid and said, "I didn't know you played quarterback in high school." "Ah heck," the kid says, "I was too small and couldn't throw the ball." He knew. I didn't have to tell him. He knew.

With this philosophy, good coaches allow players to find their own path. They then prepare them for the game, what to expect, and turn them loose on game day. The players step forward and make immediate on-field adjustments to unexpected developments as the game progresses. To the novice this may sound logical, but it is actually seldom practiced at any level of football. Coaches, in general, want control of the game in their hands. John has relinquished much of this control to his trained players, thereby allowing them to develop and flourish as emerging leaders. He flips the pyramid upside down, preparing and serving those who are above him on the field and his fellow coaches.

"I never felt, individual to individual,
that we were more talented than the other team.
We were equally talented . . .
the advantages we had were
John's coaching, execution,
and we believed in ourselves."
—Joe Mucha

41

Denny Schleper. (Courtesy Denny Schleper)

D ENNY SCHLEPER TOLD HOW HIS FOOTBALL experience under John Gagliardi influenced his attitude in a business career:

It didn't really hit me till my senior year. . . . We were going to kick off that year playing Saint Cloud State, which was in a different division, higher division, than us. Their linemen outweighed us twenty to thirty pounds per person, and by all rights we should never have been on the same field. While preparing for that game, it really struck me through meetings and discussions with John that his full intent was—and it wasn't outwardly but a very quiet type of sense—that we were going to win that game. Probably at that time, if I was honest with myself, I was saying there is not a chance in hell that we are going to win this game. I stepped back at that point and realized it is how John approaches everything—this aspect of giving you this sense you're going to win. I took that away from the Saint John's football experience in everything I do, saying, "I'm going to win." But any of these comments, if you take them just isolated, you're going to give somebody the wrong impression. They have to come with the other aspects. If your attitude is such that you're always going to win, it could be perceived as negative because it could offend a lot of people, especially in the business environment, if that is your attitude. Other things need to come along with that . . . what I practice is a quiet aggressiveness, a quiet confidence. Early in my business career I would see those terms pop up in written evaluations of myself.

Denny Schleper. (Courtesy Saint John's University)

42

Brandon Novak added this:

You always got that sense from John that this is what is supposed to happen: The Johnnies are down by ten in the fourth quarter at Saint John's. You expect a great comeback! It's like the mystique or miracles of Yankee Stadium . . . we will find a way.

Jeff Korsmo referred to this attitude as "a humble confidence" and added:

When you play for him [John] and walk out onto that field on Saturday, you're not arrogant about it, but you feel (a) I've got the best preparation; (b) I come from a great tradition that knows how to win; (c) I've got a coach on the sideline that has seen everything there is to see; and (d) I'm not walking into the game as banged up as can be. I feel great walking into the game because I haven't knocked the daylights out of myself all week [a reference to no-contact practices].

This quiet, humble confidence is noticeably prominent in the lives of ex-Johnny players. Jeff explained:

Developing your own path, not following the way everybody else does it—it's really a valuable lesson learned. I think most all of us that have ever played for him [John] agree that it has some value. He has brought this to our lives, and it continues to make a difference as we get older. . . . In whatever walk of life we're in, I think those of us that have experienced someone like John are more comfortable [with their own path]. It doesn't mean you're a maverick, but I'm more comfortable if I have a sound set of principles and values that are guiding me. If the way I'm doing something doesn't match up exactly with the way everyone else is doing it, that's fine. I have every bit as much chance at being successful with it. There's nothing wrong with going a path that is a little less traveled, and we'll end up at the same place or a little better place. I think a lot of guys that played for John, whether they will stop to recognize it or not, he has had that kind of impact on us.

Tom Linnemann offered this observation: "It doesn't matter if in high school you were eight and two or two and eight. You walk onto campus at Saint John's and you're on a winning team." John builds individuals' self-confidence subtly through film sessions. Proper blocking technique is learned and reinforced by watching game films of former teams. Films that date as far back as the 1950s are shown to current teams. A play from the archived film will be run over and over again to reinforce proper technique. While technique is being taught to current players, another subtle form of instilling self-confidence is present as well. John uses the film to instruct technique but then goes further and talks about the individual making the textbook block and against whom it was made. Typically it was a smaller lineman up against an individual of greater stature.

Mike Grant quotes John as saying, "None of these guys had big S's on their chest [Superman reference]. They were just guys from Holdingford, Avon, Little Falls . . . they were just guys that did what we asked them to do." Kurt Ramler said, "At Saint John's they believe they are going to win." Brandon Novak commented, "Will we always win? No. Will we always be in a position to win and have a chance? Yes!"

Those film sessions were important. According to Fred Cremer, "Monday film sessions involved a lot of teaching." However, film sessions were not always a pleasant affair. Each play was run over and over again, looking at the action of each position player. John Agee said, "A lot of individual instruction happened during film session." If a player performed as he was supposed to, it was acknowledged and complimented by the coaching staff. If a mental mistake was made by a player, it would be pointed out for all team members to see. Fred quoted John Gagliardi as saying, "It's not the great plays you make; it's the mistakes you don't make."

Joe Mucha described these sessions: "Film sessions can be humorous. You would be laughing sometimes [at other players' mistakes], but you knew your time in the barrel was coming because in four plays you knew you screwed up, and it would be brutal." Kurt Ramler said, "At times ninety-nine guys are laughing their tails off and one guy is feeling like a mouse." Joe Mucha qualified that: "Even when an individual messed up, John wouldn't take away your self-esteem and get you to doubt your abilities. It was used as a teaching opportunity. Film sessions were business, but dignity and self-esteem were never taken away."

John Agee spoke in agreement:

> There would be no place to hide if there was a blown assignment. There were some people he could ride harder than others, some people with whom he would use more sugar than salt. It depended on the player. He's a psychologist. It was never personal [pause] ever. It was the objectivity of how are you performing.

Fred Cremer.
(Courtesy Saint
John's University)

Fred Cremer recounted how he lost his starting spot for a time after some poor performances. "I never, ever felt I was not a good football player or a good person. It was I needed more seasoning or learning of the system. It was never a chastisement. Always positive things to correct your errors." Corrections in film sessions were often made with subtle humor or by a physical "hands-on" during practice sessions, literally walking through a play with the players. Fred carried these lessons into the classroom by being "respectful of individuals" and having "a positive attitude" toward students.

Adam Herbst spoke about the film sessions and how they related to his business environment. "You need to provide good feedback. Whether it's positive, whether it's

Adam Herbst during a game. (Courtesy Saint John's University)

45

constructive, it needs to be timely and it needs to be specific. People want that. They want to know how they're doing." He went on to point out how we have a tendency to reward and acknowledge only the star plays and how we need to reward the average and the above average as well. He related this to watching a game film and how not every play was a touchdown. Many plays were three- to five-yard gains and were acknowledged as successful plays, with individual accomplishments recognized before all the players. "Players liked that."

Personal responsibility is what John Agee learned from John's methods:

> You had to know what you were supposed to do, and do it. The thing he [John] would get most upset about, and the thing that would lead you to going on the bench, was the mental mistakes. If you physically couldn't make the play, that was different. If you blew an assignment, he was all over you.

Bernie Archbold. (Courtesy Saint John's University)

Bernie Archbold expressed the long-term impact being a part of John's team had on him:

> I quake sometimes and wonder what my life would be like if I hadn't played football. . . . I just think the discipline, the pride I found in participating . . . there's just a sense of place up there that gives me great pride to have been a part of it. . . . There is an overwhelming spirit in the football program. The recognition of what it has been over the years and how many young men have participated and come out with what I think is the same feeling I have for it. I've never had a chance to talk to anybody about that and frankly had never thought about the impact it may have had on my psyche. I do think it is something significant, to me at least, and it's probably a total intangibility for anybody else to get a grip on that or to even agree that it is a real thing. In

my mind it is, but I question that a lot of people that didn't play would see why that made any difference. . . . I take great pride in that. . . . John has kind of an intangible effect on the program . . . we all know it is because of John and his dedication to football.

"Teams didn't necessarily like playing Saint John's, but they knew it would be a clean game. We wanted to win, and wanted to win the right way."
—Joe Mucha

Instilling a strong moral character seems to be a natural consequence of being a player under John Gagliardi's coaching. During the first few weeks of practice every fall, a norm of proper behavior was established. John had discussions with his players on this, but it appeared that much of the norm was taught by upperclassmen to underclassmen. There was no formal direction from the coaching staff to the upperclassmen on this issue; they just did it. Tom Linnemann had this to say:

Maybe some guy back in 1953 was the first guy that came up with the crazy concept: to be nice to people. Wherever it started, it certainly is a rotating thing. . . . It's about creating that culture and having us fit into it.

From discussions with the interviewees, it was clear that this informal process has gone on for decades. John posted no formal list of proper and improper behaviors, but only teaching moments, to get his points

Tom Linnemann. (Courtesy Saint John's University)

across. Upperclassmen taught underclassmen by modeling and, if necessary, speaking to an underclassman about an issue. According to Denny Schleper, "The expectation level was so high it wasn't discussed as much as you think it might have been." Mike Grant stated that within a very short time as an incoming freshman, he said to himself, "This is how we are, and this is who I am now." Tom Linnemann put it this way: "As a freshman you are learning it, as a sophomore it is reinforced, and as a junior and senior you are enforcing it."

John appeared to start this process and then let it unfold, as explained by Tom Linnemann:

> In a lot of other schools they haze freshmen, all this crazy stuff . . . and mean stuff. He [John] makes a big point that "that will never happen." Freshmen hear that; it is in one of the first couple of practices. He [John] will say, "We will not do any of that garbage. That's not how we do things. You're going to feel valued; if you're not feeling valued, come let me know. That's how we work." You hear that as freshmen and your fears are somewhat alleviated. Here is the leader putting this down. As seniors we already know it because we've heard the speech three times, but we remember as freshmen being more relaxed.

Tom supervises personnel in his work, including interns. He reflects now and understands that John was "providing a framework" when giving various short, humorous talks to the team. Tom, in working with his business team, now establishes the same guidelines of "setting expectations" in regard to behavior. "You wouldn't think in a grown-up job that it would need to come out, but it absolutely does."

Brandon Novak, who still works in athletics as wrestling coach and assistant football coach, added this on the subject of behavior:

> We want men that don't need rules, and then they buy into it. You walk through our locker rooms and stuff is lying out—iPods and such. They're going to be there when they come back. You walk through the dorms, and the dorm rooms are unlocked when they go to class. It's because they have neighbors. Part of it is John; part of it is the Benedictine feel because of the monastery on campus. This is our community, these are our neighbors.

Teaching moments. John "constantly talked about succeeding in life," according to Fred Cremer. Many times it was "an ancillary thing to something that just happened" either in practice or in a film session. Denny Schleper observed that John "never had an agenda about moral, ethical issues." Much of this type of discussion occurred at Monday film sessions. Denny went on to say: "At Monday film sessions you never knew where it was going to go, you had no idea where it came from, and you had no idea when it was going to end. He covered all the things he felt he needed to." Brandon Novak commented, "He's been around and raised children . . . it's more of a conversation than a scolding."

Fred Cremer, class of 1967, described these sessions:

> You learned about self-discipline, to be respectful to others and yourself, try not to make mistakes, learn from your mistakes—these are the things that make for a successful life. Football is a microcosm of life. You walked away from film sessions learning something about football, but you also learned something else.

John Agee added this admonition stressed by John: "Don't try to upstage your opponent" with attention-seeking antics. As Kurt Ramler put it, "Don't showboat. Hand the ball to the ref."

Tom Linnemann recalled one particular film session:

> I remember watching film, and someone scored and did a little dance. John rewound it [and played it] I bet fifteen times. And each time he had a comment. "Why would you do this? This is ridiculous! This is embarrassing! What were you trying to prove?" That sucked for that person, but I guarantee every one of the other two hundred players knew they would never, ever do that.

Mike Grant told what he has adopted from his college football career as he works as a high school coach and teacher:

> When I see my people walking down the hallway, I know what I want to see—how they treat people. We better be one way. This

Mike Grant. (Courtesy Saint John's University)

vision is taught through modeling from coaching staff to students and from team leaders to underclassmen. We constantly speak during film sessions and practices about how we act and continually talk about doing the right thing. This is not a separate agenda item. I talk at various opportunities about how we act, and we won't tolerate this or that. And this is just how we are. Practices are conversations. We have an obligation to preach to young men about how to treat women, behavior in the lunchroom, how to behave to each other, about the decisions we make, and to continually talk about doing the right things. This is part of what we are and what we do.

Regarding problem students, Mike asserted that "kids that are out of control can't make it in our culture, and they get no positive feedback. They almost get shunned if they are doing the wrong thing."

Fred Cremer said this about his time at Saint John's:

At the time you don't even think about it . . . no matter what you do, you have to have some sort of organization or a code by which you are going to function. After four years [at Saint John's] you would incorporate this, and then, whatever you do, you go out into the world and apply it.

"Is this the right thing to do?" was a constant question asked by Joe Mucha at executive meetings with his colleagues at General Mills. With the foundation of his youth, he was able to advance to the position of vice-president of Human Resources. "It gave hope to tons of others," he said, speaking of those trying to do the right thing and still advancing their career.

Bernie Archbold said of John Gagliardi's expectations of players: "He expected us to know that." John would say: "You're men, you're grown up, old enough to know better. You know the things you're supposed to do and the things you aren't supposed to do."

Adam Herbst recounted an incident about a rival team coming to play one Saturday.

> T-shirts were being distributed around campus with some negative connotations about the competitor written on them. I remember that used to really upset John. Then John found out that someone on the team was involved with the production of these shirts. I remember him addressing the entire team. It's about just doing the right thing.

Fred Cremer told of a personal moment with John and how things were conducted at an individual level by the coach.

> When I was a sophomore, I took a PT class from John. I don't know why I took it. I was an English major and an education minor. I don't know why I took it. Maybe for a few extra credits, and I thought it would be fun to be around John during the winter session. This was a two-day-a-week class, or two hours a week. I don't know what happened, but by the end of the semester I started cutting his class. It was during the off season, so I didn't see John much except for that class. All of a sudden he appears at my dorm room with a knock on the door, and it's him. I knew what this was all about, and I knew I was in deep manure. He came in and was very kind, very soft-spoken, very respectful. He asked, "Why haven't you been in class?" I didn't have an answer. And then he asked, "How about your other classes? Are you cutting your other classes too?" I assured him I wasn't, but obviously he had already checked and knew I wasn't cutting them. It went on and on. We probably spent an hour talking, and in the end it was the idea that cutting his class was not the end of the world. But if I cut his class, then it [might be] British Literature, then American Literature, then all of sudden I'd start cheating on myself taking short-cuts. And he [John] was just applying it to life. That was it. I never cut

51

his class again, and I seldom cut any of my classes the rest of my four years at Saint John's . . . and it was never mentioned again. . . . I liked him, loved him, respected him.

John Gagliardi still teaches a class on campus titled "Theory of Coaching Football," and it is a student favorite.

Fred provided a simple statement: "You can show them [students] and do it in a way where you want them to be better." Brandon Novak added, "People are inherently good and want to do right. I have the same philosophy as John."

John Agee spoke about the path of his business career. What was notable about this was the cordial nature of his discussion in relation to his employers. He concluded, "I found my way to companies that share my core beliefs."

Kurt Ramler described how John changed his life. Kurt was coaching on the East Coast after graduation when his father became ill. He left his coaching position and came back home to care for his father.

In the fall, I wanted to coach. I contacted John and he let me . . . he didn't have to. I couldn't offer that much. I couldn't be there during the week all that much. I think I was up there twice a week for practices and then on weekends. He didn't need me, but I think he understood how much I needed that. I wouldn't be here today if it wasn't for that experience. I was learning from them and their philosophy. That was huge.

Kurt Ramler, hurdling an opponent. (Courtesy Saint John's University)

3

Being Prepared and Other Concepts of Football and Life

Being Prepared

It is a practice for college sports opponents to exchange game films prior to meeting on the field. These films are typically shot from several angles and are the same ones used to critique the players' performance. Film analysis occupies a large amount of time for all coaches. Typically, when a coach is not busy recruiting, he's watching game films of upcoming opponents. When the season starts and coaching is added to the schedule, little time is left for much of a personal life. Games are typically played on Saturday afternoons. On Monday nights, film of the previous week's game is reviewed by the players. Before practice on Monday and Tuesday, the game film of the upcoming opponent has already been analyzed, and a rough game plan is starting to take shape. Old game films from the opposing team also have some use, but film of the last week's game is more relevant. Much time is spent studying the play of both teams.

Bernie Archbold elaborated on this important topic of studying game films:

We saw game film till we were blind. Frontwards and backwards. . . . If you made a mistake during a game, you really didn't want to be alive that next week when [we] did films, because he [John] would be on that spot and go back and forth, back and forth. That was a good teaching aid as it turned out. . . . A leader or a boss or a manager or a coach certainly has some responsibility to his people, and sometimes it is going to be unpleasant but needs to be done. You have to do it. I don't think I necessarily got that from John, but maybe he reinforced it.

Tom Linnemann, a quarterback, told how John's methods of preparation for a game influenced him:

Tom Linnemann. (Courtesy Saint John's University)

The way he prepares you is very cerebral. It isn't a rah-rah thing, jumping up and down. John would ask a lot of questions to see what I was thinking. I spent three hours a day watching film with various coaches. He [John] put such a premium on knowledge going in. When you're in a game, things are going to happen, and game plans can go out the window very quickly. But if you prepare for every possible scenario on Monday, Tuesday, Wednesday, Thursday, and Friday for Saturday, in your head you're able to make these decisions as the game plan changes. You can execute rather than wasting a quarter trying to figure out how you're going to execute. . . . I mentored a high school quarterback and used the same methods John did. We watched films and I asked a lot of questions. What would you do here? What's this? What's that? Preparing him for that game.

54

Brandon Novak voiced a similar theme: "Football is the greatest scheming game ever invented. It's a chess match. When you slack and don't put the work in on the front end, you're going to be in trouble on the back end."

Regarding game preparation and psychology, Jeff Korsmo stated, "The intensity of the preparation was almost inversely related to the strength of the opponent." This was in relation to how hard John would drive the team during the week leading up to game day. Jeff continued along the same line:

> John had a great deal of insight into human behavior and psychology. He knew his real job was for us to be all the way there [mentally] for the teams we ought to beat handily. If anything, he was holding the reins back for the teams he figured we would be worked up for. . . . It was all about preparing for that week's team. Then during film session, the bigger the win, the harder he was on [us]. He knew he had to find ways to bring [us] back to earth.

The 1976 National Champion winners. (Courtesy Saint John's University)

55

Joe Mucha explained John's work ethic regarding preparation. John "would watch more game film than any of the assistants, and by Monday morning have a game plan in place for a week of practice." By game day, Joe added, "we were very prepared and knew what the opponent was probably going to do . . . when the ball was snapped. . . . [We] could almost see what was going to happen." John would put people "in the right position, [but] it was still up to the individual to make the play." John Agee said, "John's work ethic is notorious. He outworks everybody. His teams are better prepared from an intellectual point of view."

The theme of preparation was also recalled by Bernie Archbold. He spoke of John's total dedication to coaching and his requirement that we view it the same way.

> . . . it isn't just during the football season. I got the feeling that before and after the football season, [John Gagliardi] was still thinking about football. . . . We would run certain plays over and over again—repetition, repetition, repetition. We might have thought we were doing a good job. I guess I learned from that, that we weren't doing as good a job as we thought we were, and you can't ever work too hard to do things right and achieve whatever level of excellence John wanted for us. . . . I would like to lead by example [in my business career]. I figured I had to be the best producer. I should be the hardest worker, the first one there in the morning, the last one there at night. . . . John put in way more hours than anyone of us would think.

Joe Mucha told a story of walking by John's office one day during the winter. "John was watching films, but then I noticed the jersey numbers didn't match up with the past season's players." Joe then realized that the film was not of the current season but of sometime in the past. John sat there analyzing the film and "coaching the individuals like a film session in the film room."

Game Planning

ALL THE PLAYERS INTERVIEWED AT SOME POINT gave testament to the absolute brilliance and innovation of game-planning by John Gagliardi. Statements to the press could be of contrary nature and at first glance seemed to suggest that John would be unprepared for the next game. Mike Grant quoted John: "We don't know what we're going to do against next week's opponent. They're pretty good with some great players." Mike thought that this was an effort at "masking his intellectual ability." Denny Schleper referred to this as "humbleness" on John's part and a "characteristic makeup." In reality, Denny said that it went back to the "quiet confidence" John exhibited. Denny offered this example:

> A phrase he [John] repeatedly gave to us, and I actually use it still in our firm, is the comment "We are very ordinary people, we do very

John discussing a play from a 3 x 5 card with Rick Bell. (Courtesy Saint John's University)

ordinary things. We just have to do them in an extraordinary way." Even from a business perspective, when you really dig down to it, what we do are very simple things. So what is going to separate all of us? That goes back to the comment of doing the basic things, the little things, in an extraordinary way. In the business world, I realized it was the simple things—returning a phone call or returning an e-mail quickly. [What you do] can be that simple [and yet] be viewed as extraordinary. Too many people concentrate on really trying to stand out, and most of us can't do that. We really just need to concentrate on those ordinary things and doing them in an extraordinary way.

"John prepared me to succeed," Tom Linnemann claimed, "and then gave me the control and the autonomy to succeed." Tom compared the preparation for a game to that of many things in business. His point of comparison was that the work leading up to the game exceeded that of the actual game. "You don't get a redo" if things don't go well or if you don't have the needed answers to relevant questions. "Here's your shot. Do it." He went on to say: "I'm in business [Target Corporation] and it's competitive by nature. Having that preparedness builds trust in the people you're talking to."

Reinventing the Team and Game-Scheming

Every year some starting players graduate. The talent pool is ever changing. John Gagliardi has won four national championships, and, according to Joe Mucha, "each of them was different in culture and style." Some teams had great offenses, and some had great defenses. John's "genius is reinventing himself with who he had" according to Joe. Bernie Archbold (class of 1958) summed up what he thought was John's theory about passing during his career as a quarterback: "Very rarely did we pass. For two reasons: it wasn't in John's philosophy, and I wasn't a good passer." That philosophy was to change, and Saint John's passing game would surpass that of the competition in the decades going forward.

Live game-time reinvention was an ongoing element of Johnny games. John Agee related this to a career:

> John will ask the players during the game or at halftime: "What is this guy doing to you? What do you think would work? How do you think you could have an advantage?" As opposed to always dictating. That is something you carry with you in your life. And so you say: "What are the subordinates saying? What good ideas do they have? Isn't it better to surface those ideas rather than dictate what you think is always best?"

Every week also saw reinvention. "John would come to practice every week with a different set of cards," according to John Agee. These would be new plays he had devised for the coming week's opponent. They would be similar to but slightly different than those used previously.

John also tries to reinvent his teams to be on the leading edge of football theory. Kurt Ramler discussed this aspect:

> John's philosophy lends itself to getting better recruits. There is no hitting in practice. There are really very few people that enjoy that . . . mandatory conditioning, run till you puke. Nobody likes that, and they don't do them at Saint John's. So he has created this environment which allows for him to have more talent. I learned from John it's okay to say "To heck with what other people think." Conventional wisdom is sometimes, sometimes is really stupid. People say, "You gotta do it this way." No you don't. "You have to condition." No you don't. "You have to lift." No you don't. You take that twenty minutes of conditioning and you get twenty more reps [of practice plays]. It's good to think of new things and practice them. There are three programs in America that do things the way we do philosophically: ours, Saint John's, and Eden Prairie High School.

Joe Mucha worked for General Mills most of his career and incorporated John's constant reinvention:

> If things are going good, somebody [a competitor] is eventually going to figure out why. What's the next step of being better than where you are right now? You would intellectually create a dissonance. What is the

next step? What is the next step to be ahead of everyone else? In the business world our customers are changing, and their objectives are changing. The training we do has to match up to where the customer is going to be. Are you bringing along the skills of your people to match the business environment that is always changing? It's hard to get people to change when things are going well. It's easy to change in crisis. You have to make adjustments before your competitor does because they have smart people too.

Adam Herbst considers John Gagliardi a "pioneer of film study." John's ability to change is witnessed by changes in using different film methods—splicing film together for many years, and now using computer technology for film studies. It demonstrated to Adam "the importance of accepting change," even for a guy in his seventies or eighties.

Brandon Novak put John's work strategies in simple terms: "Get rid of the big boulders first. Don't let stuff pile up. Cut out the unnecessary, and simplify the process."

Humor

HUMOR IS A THEME THAT WAS brought up by many people. John Agee said that John understood that football was "serious business, but it's still just a game." According to Fred Cremer, many times John would pull the whole team together at the end of practice and tell a humorous story or a few jokes. "We would leave practice laughing." But come game time, it was "taking care of business," with little humor. Fred saw in John a tendency to make fun of himself at times. As a career teacher, Fred learned that it was okay to make fun of yourself in front of a class. In fact, it "opened up opportunities later on to subtly make fun of others." It helped open a positive window for dialogue that wasn't there before.

John gives a limited number of speeches to groups across the country and non-profits in the university area. I was in his office one day when he was preparing for a speech at an award presentation. What was most remarkable was his notes, which consisted of a series of one-word topics. John said, "I can't write a speech. I just get a few thoughts, and from there who knows where I'm going to go? That's my style." John's wife, Peggy, agreed:

> I'll ask him how it went, and he'll say, "It went really well, but I didn't use what I thought I was going to use." He gets there, and he doesn't know which direction it's going to go. He can't memorize it.

Mike Grant made this comment about John's use of humor:

> At Saint John's you liked going to practice and hang out with a bunch of your brothers. People would come early and stay late. We loved it. To do this and still win is the art of coaching. To know when to tell jokes and take it down a notch. At the end of practice John sometimes does a game of "Simon Says." He loves to do that. We would laugh so hard we would just cry at the jokes he would tell. They are the lamest jokes, but his knack of timing, and the art—he could have been a comedian.

John and Mike Grant during a game. (Courtesy Saint John's University)

Denny Schleper told about a practice session when John used some slight self-deprecating humor. It was toward midseason when the offensive team was running through a series of new plays for use against the upcoming opponent. John would call out a play for the offense to run, and then observe the dry run for miscues. He seemed to have a problem that day remembering what plays he had instituted earlier in the week for the upcoming opponent and would call out plays from previous opponents. Denny, the quarterback, would call an audible for what he thought John really wanted, and then run the play. John then called a play that was run against an opponent a long time in the past. The offensive team all looked at each other, not really sure what to think. They ran what they thought John wanted. As the play was finishing, they could see John coming straight toward them with a purpose, hat thrown on the ground. As John came closer, they detected that he had a slight smirk on his face. John then said, "How do you know what I want when I don't even know what I want?"

Humor is a part of John's repertoire, and all former players agreed that they could not come close to duplicating what he did. What they recognized, though, was the importance of humor in their continuing daily lives.

At some point, usually while talking about humor, former players would do a vocal and sometimes a physical impression of John. It would usually be a humorous one-liner. If imitation is truly the greatest form of flattery, John has many admirers.

Assessment of Individuals

WITH NO CONTACT IN PRACTICES and no junior varsity games, assessment of individuals was made in a variety of ways, one of these being soliciting the opinion of starters. John Agee said, "He [John] would ask the starters who the good young players were that were playing opposite them." With this method, it was evident to everyone: "When you have your chance, you have to take advantage of it," according to Tom Linnemann. The importance of doing one's best on game film was paramount. This has resulted in some rather lopsided scores at times, for even a fifth or sixth stringer wants to show ability on game film.

Denny Schleper spoke of individual assessment and how he applied another aspect of it in his business career at LarsonAllen:

> In the early years John didn't have many assistants, so he would have to make many of the ability assessments by himself, and often very quickly. Once off the A list, it is tough to get back on. There was one guy that through some injuries was given an opportunity as a senior to get back on the A list. He was a running back, but his specialty was his blocking skills. John's comment was, "I thought this guy was going to amount to nothing, and here he turns into a guy that I'm going to be showing his blocking skills for the next twenty years through film to players." What it told me was that even someone like Gagliardi can't handpick those talents, and people change. In our organization we have people come in and sometimes they struggle. Many times people will say, "This person will never make it." And I say, "You're not good enough to judge that. I'm not good enough to judge that. Let's just keep giving them a shot, and maybe they won't make it, but they could also be one of those stars, so let's be careful."

Joe Mucha told how forming a good team in the marketplace has similarities to forming a good working combination on a football team:

> Sometimes it was not the best marketer, but it was the best marketer that worked with the salesperson that got us the best result, rather than the marketer that was worried about his next assignment and how he could become CEO. As individuals in an organization, you think your mission is to maximize the market. Yours is to maximize sales, yours is to maximize financial, but if we work together we can optimize. We may not maximize our functions, but if we work together, we can optimize the potential of the organization. That is John Gagliardi in his coaching style. The best two are not always on the field, but the best two that work together.

John Agee encapsulated a key to success in business: "Almost always it isn't about numbers; it comes down to people. More than anything else, the key to success was evaluating people and making a judgment."

Open-Door Policy

JOHN GAGLIARDI'S OFFICE IS ALONG a row of offices on the top floor of the Warner Palaestra building. It is relatively spacious, approximately ten by twenty feet. It has windows and contains typical university furniture. Kurt Ramler said, "We used to call his office 'The Black Hole.' You had to walk by his office fast or you get sucked in, and you'd be in there for an hour minimum, which was fun." Joe Mucha adopted this simple but important concept in his business career and arranged his office to be more inviting. He removed curtains from glass walls and made sure that he faced people coming in.

According to Tom Linnemann, John is an "older coach, but not old school. He has kept a part of himself open to the eighteen- to twenty-two-year-olds. He finds a way to relate to them, mostly by asking questions." Joe Mucha said that John understands what motivates each generation. "He is more modern than thirty-year-old coaches." Brandon Novak said, "He's eighteen at heart because that is who he is dealing with." Joe Mucha brought this mindset into his work career and "tried to understand each generation and what motivates them."

Jim Gagliardi agreed with these views:

> You're always around eighteen- to twenty-two-year-old kids. I understand why my dad has stayed so young. You never feel like you're grown up. . . . I feel like I'm part of them, except I don't know how to text as well.

Short Memory on Mistakes

Learn from mistakes but don't dwell on it" was something Joe Mucha learned. After a loss, they thought they were going to have a difficult film session, but instead, after a very brief time, John moved on. Joe recalled a time in his business career when a very unpleasant layoff was required. "Once cutbacks were completed and people treated right as best we could, we moved on, looked forward, and focused on the future."

Jeff Korsmo repeated the same lesson, which he learned from watching a game film of a poor performance. He related it to his current life at the Mayo Clinic:

> It's really helped me, especially in roles like I'm in today, where there's a huge amount of things you're responsible for and not everything goes the way you would like. If you don't do that [learning from mistakes but not dwelling on them], you'll drag yourself down over time.

Vision

Vision is an all-encompassing theme that was repeated in various forms. Mike Grant stated:

> Leaders like John have to have their handprint on everything. They have a great vision and can convey that vision. How he wants his players to act in school, on the field, perform. How you handle yourself when you score a touchdown. John has a vision of what this should look like and will not delegate this entirely to assistants. The great leaders like John, when they walk, can see everything that is going on, from the minutest little detail. And they see it, and they either approve or disapprove, and over time everything that is happening is not by accident. This is true in corporate leadership. The great ones have a vision as they walk the corridors or go onsite. They have a vision of what it should look like. The great ones can convey that vision so people act on it, and when they are successful, they believe in it even more.

4

Lasting Impressions

As quoted earlier, Bernie Archbold made the following comments about having played for John Gagliardi. He spoke of

the recognition of what it has been over the years and how many young men have participated and come out with what I think is the same feeling I have for it. I've never had a chance to talk to anybody about that and frankly had never thought about the impact it may have had on my psyche. I do think it is something significant, to me at least, and it's probably a total intangibility for anybody else to get a grip on that or even to agree that it is a real thing.

The modeling conducted by Coach John Gagliardi to his players over the last six decades has affected his players in a positive way. The alumni benefited directly from their relationship to John. Not all ex-players applied the same elements in their lives that they learned from John, but all applied at least some. Many alumni credited their family, as well as other individuals, for their leadership development. All credited John, to some degree, with instilling these elements in their lives.

When John's players graduated from Saint John's University, they were at a higher level in the leadership hierarchy than if they had not played football under John. In essence, the players stepped out of the football program after four years with skills to be more effective leaders.

The Benedictines and John Gagliardi

W OULD THE FORMER PLAYERS have responded similarly if they had just attended the university and not played football? Did their growth come from John Gagliardi's influence or from the university? I believe the answer is: both. Joe Mucha said, "John teaches how great Benedictines would want all men to live their lives. John teaches it, but his form is football." Bernie Archbold said, "He is part of the big picture [with reference to the institution of Saint John's]. It isn't the big picture that is part of him."

Jeff Korsmo had further comment on this topic:

He [John] was influenced by the Benedictines as well. They weren't totally inseparable, and that's the Benedictine humility, service, simplicity, and hospitality. I think all those things were quite consistent with what you saw out of the Benedictine monks. For the most part, what you saw out of John's program is quite complementary in that sense. For a football program it was as hospitable as you could imagine. It was simple in most ways. It expected a high level of dedication and was kind of service-orientated in a sense.

There is ample evidence that exposure to John had an impact beyond what non-player students experienced. The type of modeling that John exhibited takes time to acquire, and for the most part he was the one faculty member modeling most to the former players. Other faculty members modeled to these same former players as well, but the exposure to John represented a significant portion of football players' time at Saint John's. Korsmo put it this way: "If I had been in Axel Theimer's choir, maybe I would have answered these questions with

'This is Axel's expression of the Benedictine Rule.'" The institution of Saint John's, as a whole, has influenced students' lives, and John has modeled that behavior to some degree directly to those who played football. The *quality* of time is measured by the *quantity* with which one spends it. It is difficult to lead; it is even more difficult to train your followers to become leaders.

Leadership Training

JOHN GAGLIARDI HAS HAD A MAJOR IMPACT on the lives of former players. One of the elements that they have taken with them is very subtle and not easily recognized at first glance. Coach Gagliardi prepares his players for games, and then lets them go to do the business that he has prepared them for. This type of responsibility being released to individuals is uncommon in modern sports. This operating philosophy may well be a tactical move to help the team win, but it has also developed a very positive side-effect on the culture of the program and how individuals mature into leaders. A unique culture has continually developed

John. (Courtesy John Biasi)

within the program. As players develop and become leaders, they enforce an ongoing cycle within the team. They simply believe this is their team, and they will do what is necessary to improve, protect, and enrich the unit. What may be a tactical advantage on the football field is also a superior leadership training program.

Summary

IF ASKED HOW HE LEADS, JOHN GAGLIARDI couldn't tell us, for he does it in a way that is natural for him. Still, several points on leadership emerged as key for John:

- The fundamental belief in and the personal operating philosophy of the Golden Rule;
- High intelligence overall, and particularly in his field of work, a broad-ranging curiosity combined with a creative mind;
- Diminished ego;
- A relentless focus on all aspects of the job at hand; distractions outside of this world are not tolerated (including one's own ego);
- Family at 360 degrees;
- Prepare your people and then let them run.

Individuals who are very good at their professions do their work in a fluid motion that appears to the rest of us as effortless. It may appear to the casual bystander that they are hardly working. In fact, their mind is running full out, and their synapses are firing in perfect rhythm, for they are "in the zone"—a painter, a poet, a welder, a teacher, a quarterback, or an organizational leader. If you think this is only a story of how to lead a sports team, read it again. For within lies the blueprint of leadership in all of us.

Final Thoughts

THE "HAIL MARY PASS" IS A FOOTBALL TERM used to describe a long forward pass that has only a prayer's chance of completion. It is an "against all odds" moment. The ball is in the air for what seems an eternity. Hearts pound, muscles tense, the mind is tightly focused . . . yet the quiet is deafening. No one breathes during this time—not players, benchwarmers, coaches, family, fans—the chances of success are so slim . . . but on occasion . . .

There are rare times when someone is hired to lead and everything comes together. It is just the right fit, a one in a million. Organization and individual seemingly meld with distinction. Somebody gives them a chance, and they run with it. Hearts pound, muscles tense, and the mind focuses. And once again, the quietness is deafening . . . the chances of success are slim . . . but on occasion . . . AVE MARIA!

John's Final Comment

SOMEBODY ASKED ME WHEN WE WON the national championship (2003) and broke the record (most wins) if I thought that someday I would do this. When I came here (to Saint John's), I was a twenty-six-year-old guy, and all I had on my mind after I spotted that good-looking student nurse up at the hospital was, "How could I get a date with that gal?" How could I possibly think that someday I would be married to her for over fifty years, and we would have nineteen grandchildren? She would be a seventy-year-old grandmother, and the most incredible part of all, she would still look real good to me. How can you even think in those kinds of terms? I've never really had a goal or a dream. I just do the best I can."

Appendix

College Football's 300 Win Club (at completion of the 2009 season)
There have been more than 25,000 head coaches in the history of college football. Only ten of these have won more than 300 games.

1. John Gagliardi, SJU: 471-126-11, 61 years, .784 (active)
2. Eddie Robinson, Grambling: 408-165-15, 55 years, .707
3. Joe Paterno, Penn State: 394-129-3, 43 years, .752 (active)
4. Bobby Bowden, Florida State: 389-129-4, 43 years, .749
5. Paul "Bear" Bryant, Alabama: 323-85-17, 38 years, .780
6. Glenn "Pop" Warner, Temple: 319-106-32, 44 years, .733
7. Roy Kidd, Eastern Kentucky: 315-123-8, 39 years, .715
8. Amos Alonzo Stagg, Pacific: 314-199-35, 57 years, .605
9. Frosty Westering, Pacific Lutheran: 305-96-7, 39 years, .756
10. Tubby Raymond, Delaware: 300-119-3, 36 years, .714

John Gagliardi: Facts and Figures (at completion of the 2009 season)
Career Record: 471-126-11 (1949–present)
Career Record at Carroll (Mont.): 24-6-1 (1949–1952)
Career Record at SJU: 447-120-10 (1953–present)

John Gagliardi's Season Records

YEAR	SCHOOL	W	L	T	CONF.	POST
1949	Carroll (Mont.)	6	1	0	2nd	
1950	Carroll (Mont.)	5	2	0	1st	
1951	Carroll (Mont.)	6	1	1	1st	
1952	Carroll (Mont.)	7	2	0	1st	
1953	Saint John's (Minn.)	6	2	0	T-1st	
1954	Saint John's (Minn.)	6	2	0	N/A	
1955	Saint John's (Minn.)	7	2	0	T-2nd	
1956	Saint John's (Minn.)	3	4	1	5th	
1957	Saint John's (Minn.)	5	3	0	4th	
1958	Saint John's (Minn.)	6	2	0	3rd	
1959	Saint John's (Minn.)	5	3	0	4th	
1960	Saint John's (Minn.)	4	3	1	6th	
1961	Saint John's (Minn.)	6	2	0	T-2nd	
1962	Saint John's (Minn.)	9	0	0	1st	
1963	Saint John's (Minn.)	10	0	0	1st	NAIA Champ
1964	Saint John's (Minn.)	4	3	0	T-3rd	
1965	Saint John's (Minn.)	11	0	0	1st	NAIA Champ
1966	Saint John's (Minn.)	4	3	1	5th	
1967	Saint John's (Minn.)	3	5	0	5th	
1968	Saint John's (Minn.)	6	4	0	T-3rd	
1969	Saint John's (Minn.)	8	1	1	2nd	Mineral Bowl Champ
1970	Saint John's (Minn.)	6	3	0	N/A	
1971	Saint John's (Minn.)	8	1	0	T-1st	
1972	Saint John's (Minn.)	7	2	0	2nd	
1973	Saint John's (Minn.)	4	4	0	5th	
1974	Saint John's (Minn.)	7	2	0	T-1st	
1975	Saint John's (Minn.)	8	1	1	1st	
1976	Saint John's (Minn.)	10	0	1	1st	NCAA Nat'l Chmp
1977	Saint John's (Minn.)	7	2	0	1st	NCAA Qfinals

1978	Saint John's (Minn.)	6	3	0	4th	
1979	Saint John's (Minn.)	7	2	0	T-1st	
1980	Saint John's (Minn.)	5	3	0	3rd	
1981	Saint John's (Minn.)	7	2	0	T-2nd	
1982	Saint John's (Minn.)	9	1	0	1st	NAIA 1st Round
1983	Saint John's (Minn.)	7	4	0	2nd	
1984	Saint John's (Minn.)	6	3	0	4th	
1985	Saint John's (Minn.)	8	2	0	1st	NCAA 1st Round
1986	Saint John's (Minn.)	4	4	1	5th	
1987	Saint John's (Minn.)	8	3	0	T-2nd	NCAA Qfinals
1988	Saint John's (Minn.)	7	2	0	3rd	
1989	Saint John's (Minn.)	10	1	1	1st	NCAA Semifinals
1990	Saint John's (Minn.)	7	3	0	T-3rd	
1991	Saint John's (Minn.)	11	1	0	1st	NCAA Semifinals
1992	Saint John's (Minn.)	8	1	1	2nd	
1993	Saint John's (Minn.)	12	1	0	1st	NCAA Semifinals
1994	Saint John's (Minn.)	11	2	0	1st	NCAA Semifinals
1995	Saint John's (Minn.)	8	1	1	T-1st	
1996	Saint John's (Minn.)	11	1	0	1st	NCAA Qfinals
1997	Saint John's (Minn.)	6	4	0	4th	
1998	Saint John's (Minn.)	11	1	0	1st	NCAA Qfinals
1999	Saint John's (Minn.)	11	2	0	1st	NCAA Qfinals
2000	Saint John's (Minn.)	13	2	0	2nd	NCAA Runner-up
2001	Saint John's (Minn.)	11	3	0	T-1st	NCAA Semifinals
2002	Saint John's (Minn.)	12	2	0	1st	NCAA Semifinals
2003	Saint John's (Minn.)	14	0	0	1st	NCAA Nat'l Chmp
2004	Saint John's (Minn.)	7	3	0	2nd	
2005	Saint John's (Minn.)	11	1	0	1st	NCAA 2nd Round
2006	Saint John's (Minn.)	11	2	0	T-1st	NCAA Qfinals
2007	Saint John's (Minn.)	10	2	0	2nd	NCAA 2nd Round
2008	Saint John's (Minn.)	8	3	0	1st	NCAA 1st Round
2009	Saint John's (Minn.)	10	1	0	1st	NCAA 1st Round
TOTALS		471	126	11		

About the Author

David Weeres grew up on a small farm near Saint Nicholas in Central Minnesota. After serving as a sergeant in the United States Army, he became a commercial pilot and spent much of his career as a major airline pilot; he currently is a corporate chief pilot. For nine years he was an adjunct professor of aviation at St. Cloud State University. He has an undergraduate degree in engineering and a master's degree in aeronautical science. David holds a Doctorate of Education in Leadership from Saint Mary's University of Minnesota. He lives in Clearwater, Minnesota, with his wife Karen and children Benjamin and Heidi.